Homespun

Homespun

Ronald Spessard

John: Thank you for reading about my family! Enjoy!

Ronald Spessard

TATE PUBLISHING
AND ENTERPRISES, LLC

Homespun
Copyright © 2014 by Ronald Spessard. All rights reserved.

No part of this publication may be reproduced, stored in a retrieval system or transmitted in any way by any means, electronic, mechanical, photocopy, recording or otherwise without the prior permission of the author except as provided by USA copyright law.

The opinions expressed by the author are not necessarily those of Tate Publishing, LLC.

Published by Tate Publishing & Enterprises, LLC
127 E. Trade Center Terrace | Mustang, Oklahoma 73064 USA
1.888.361.9473 | www.tatepublishing.com

Tate Publishing is committed to excellence in the publishing industry. The company reflects the philosophy established by the founders, based on Psalm 68:11,
"The Lord gave the word and great was the company of those who published it."

Book design copyright © 2014 by Tate Publishing, LLC. All rights reserved.
Cover design by Joseph Emnace
Interior design by Jomel Pepito

Published in the United States of America

ISBN: 978-1-63185-306-7
1. Biography & Autobiography / General
14.06.02

To my relatives who taught me the true riches of life and instilled in me courage, self-reliance, and faith.

To my wife, Jamie-Ellen, and my children, Bobby Lee and Kelly Rose, with whom I continue to experience the importance of family strength and unity.

Introduction

In the interest of sharing the origins of my memories and family history, I can offer little insight into the early lives of my mother and father. I do not recall meeting my mother, Lorraine, until the summer before I entered the fourth grade. Her whereabouts and occupation during my early years was never revealed to me by any family member.

Later, I would learn that my parents were divorced before my second birthday while my mother was pregnant with my brother, Jerry. She was the only family member to be divorced.

I recall seeing my father only twice in my life, once when I was thirteen as he walked across a busy street to visit my mother and again when I was a young soldier at home on leave. My father had a new family and was very uncomfortable with me just showing up at his home and introducing myself. He became emotional and began to tear up. It was not my intent to cause my father any pain, so I told him not to be concerned about me and that everything was okay. We shook hands, and I walked away.

The earliest memory I have of a home and family was that of living with my remarkable grandparents along with four of their fourteen children who were still living at home and attending school. These four siblings would become more like my older brothers and sisters than my uncles and aunts.

My memories honor all of my family, but my mentors, during the years when our character is forged, were my grandparents and my uncles.

All of the brothers are gone now, but their lives mattered. Oh, how they mattered! By example, they taught me courage, self-reliance, manners, respect for women, and the importance of family strength and unity.

With softer and nurturing ways, my aunts would also influence my life more and more as I grew from a boy into a man. Without exception, my aunts married, raised, and educated their children, owned their homes and lived strong, independent, and loving lives.

I have listed the fourteen Carter siblings in order from eldest to youngest to make it easier for the reader to relate to my family.

Homespun

Many, many thanks to all who read my story.

Carter Siblings:
Mary
Eddie
Alvey
Jane
Lindell
Elta Mae
Lorraine
Juni
Josephine
Virginia Lee
Tempi-Glen
Sunny
Phil
Jean

Granny's Woodpile

It was a spring morning, Easter break: sunny, clear, and cool; the kind of morning that feels good to wear a flannel shirt or lightweight jacket. Granddaddy was working at the tannery, and the kids still living at home—three of the fourteen—were off to work at neighboring farms or the brickyard. Granny, with her hair pulled back into a bun and wearing a full-length blue gingham apron, was in her usual place; the kitchen, breaking kindling wood and putting it under the steel plates of the wood-burning cooking stove.

This was a pie baking day, and she opened the mason jars, removed the wax covering, and poured sour cherries, canned from last year, into a large wooden bowl.

Already, the dough had been rolled out flat and placed across four metal pie pans on the white porcelain-topped kitchen table.

She filled up the first pan with cherries, added just the right amount of sugar, and put on the top covering of dough, punching fork holes through it to keep it from boiling over. Then, she used her thumb to pinch a border tightly around the edges of the pie pan. Now, she did what I was waiting for.

She used a knife to cut away the excess dough from the edges and rolled it into a ball.

Once the pies were in the oven, Granny would take the dough balls, flatten them, fry them in an iron skillet, and serve them to me, still hot with butter and molasses. Nothing was ever wasted. What a treat!

As I began eating, a knock came from the back screen door adjoining the kitchen.

Standing there was a tall, slender, elderly man, wearing a tattered, dark brown, narrow-brimmed hat with a small blue feather in the band. His silver gray hair almost touched the shoulders of his brown and white tweed jacket, patched at the elbows. He wore gray knit gloves trimmed across the top and fingers with brown leather, worn and torn.

He tapped twice more upon the screen door with his cane.

My grandmother walked to the door and asked if she could help him.

The man politely removed his hat and asked if she could possibly have some work for him to do around the property in exchange for a meal.

This was not unusual at all in our rural community, and Granny never turned anyone away from her door hungry.

She thought for a moment and then asked the man if he would move the woodpile stacked on the porch by the cistern to a spot around the corner of the house under the grape arbor.

He nodded in agreement and, as he began to move and restack the woodpile, Granny went to the pantry, removed two large pork chops from the Crock-Pot, cleaned off the lard, and fried them up in the iron skillet along with a potato, quickly sliced, skin still on, and lightly salted.

By the time the woodpile was moved, the man's meal was ready. He ate quietly on the back porch sitting on the small bench by a table placed close to the cistern, never asking or expecting to enter the house.

When he was through, he tapped once more, lightly, upon the screen door. Granny handed him a second pork chop between two slices of freshly baked bread and wrapped in waxed paper.

The elderly man hung his cane from his arm, bowed ever so slightly, tipped his hat, and said, "Thank you, ma'am. God bless you." With that, he quickly walked away.

I asked Granny why she had him move the woodpile again. After all, I had seen this occur more than a few times.

She replied, "Ronnie, never turn an honest man away from your door hungry, or refuse his desire to work; let him keep his pride."

I looked out the back window in time to see the man disappear onto the dirt road beyond our yard.

I would never know him or see him again, but I wished him well.

Lion's Roar

Since my earliest memory, I sometimes found myself in the home and under the care of my Uncle Alvey.

Here, there were no hugs and kisses; yet, I always felt safe, happy, and cared for. As long as I followed the rules, such as respect for the elders and showing good manners, all would be well.

But should I say something inappropriate, use bad language for example, or even think of behaving poorly, Uncle Alvey, lean and tall with his intense eyes, the color of his dark hair, would thunder into the room, his voice shaking the very walls, and put everything in order very quickly.

There would not be any more chances should I fail to listen again. Should I be foolhardy—and being an active second grade boy, I sometimes was—and break one of the rules again, Aunt Dot would inform Uncle Alvey upon his return from work, and I would find myself with an early bath from two basins of water on the kitchen floor and a quick supper before going off to bed. Including his two daughters—Bonnie and Teresa, just two years younger than myself—I was one of a dozen cousins, and no one ever talked back to Uncle Alvey.

During the summer of my second grade, I was with my entire family at a church camp meeting along the banks of the Conococheague Creek with gospel hymns being sung and a huge bonfire in the center of Connie Mack Park.

I had been told not to play behind the parked cars as it was very dark, and the ground was uneven and rocky. Nevertheless, I was off—yes, behind the cars—with several other boys, running, playing tag, and wrestling. I took a tumble, the palm of my right hand falling directly onto a broken coke bottle, cutting deeply just under my thumb. The boys all ran screaming for help from the nearest adult. The hand that grabbed my shirt, none too gently, and took me to where we could use a car's headlights to assess the damage was, of course, Uncle Alvey.

Wrapping his handkerchief around my badly bleeding hand, he gruffly admonished me for not being where I was supposed to be, and to stop crying as he drove us off to awaken the town doctor in his home. Stitches would be needed. I was taken to the back door so my blood would not stain the doctor's carpets.

Homespun

There was no anesthetic or painkiller of any kind in the home, but out of the doctor's little black bag came the hooked needle and thread necessary to sew up my hand.

It would take six stitches altogether, and on the third one, I flinched and broke loose the previous one. The doctor yelled at me, "Look what you've done. Now be still!"

In an instant, Uncle Alvey roared across the room, telling the doctor in no uncertain terms, "Don't you yell at him; he is just a boy and afraid. Just get this done as quick as possible."

I was shocked and forgot my pain. Even the doctor did not talk back to Uncle Alvey. Not another word was spoken as my wound was dressed, and I was taken back to the camp meeting.

Something changed that night. I knew for the first time that Uncle Alvey loved me. With each passing year, our friendship grew and the Lion's roar faded.

He became a sought-after Master Tanner and lived his life a silent hero asking for and expecting nothing, honoring his wife and loving his daughters after having left footprints in North Africa, Italy, and Normandy, for all generations to come.

One very cold gray December day in my middle years, Uncle Alvey was taken from us by a sudden heart attack. The Lion was at peace and would roar now only in my memory.

Today, if charting an improper course, I find myself listening, almost expecting the walls to thunder again should I not set things in proper order quickly.

What a joy it was to have him in my life.

I miss him still.

Thanks for the Ride

Everyone was excited and talking at the same time on this hot summer evening. Supper was over, and about a dozen kids from our family and the neighborhood were gathered in front of my grandmother's porch. The older kids, maybe age thirteen or fourteen, would be taking us all up Town Hill to the movie house just past the square. My first movie! I had seen a TV screen once, as one of the kids in the neighborhood had one with a twelve-inch picture! But a movie? Never!

Granny and two or three aunts and uncles were grouped together on the porch steps, smiling and giving last-minute instructions about how the older kids were to watch over the younger ones. My uncle Phil's best friend, Billy, would be watching me, but not just yet.

As usual, I was finding something to play with and passing the time while we waited to leave. On the ground, I found a discarded coiled piece of sharp metal, rolled around a key which had been used to open a fresh can of coffee. I thought to myself, *How long is this strip of metal if it is unrolled and stretched all the way out?*

Without thinking about it, I held onto the loose end with one hand and quickly stretched it out to its full length with the other. Instantly, all four fingers on my right hand were cut by the razor sharp edges of metal and bleeding profusely. I was yelling and crying and already upset that now, I would miss my trip to the movie house.

Not so! Granny went into action, and within minutes, brought her box of linen bandages and iodine to the rescue. The famous box was always ready as injuries on a farm, or on butchering day, were not uncommon. Soon, each finger was bandaged tightly, and I was told to stop crying and go with the other kids. My fingers would stop hurting by the time we arrived at the movie house.

The older boys had bikes and would haul the younger kids up town. That idea worked until we crossed the stone bridge and started up Town Hill. It was so steep; we all walked up to the town square with the older boys pushing their bikes. Once at the movie house, the bikes were parked alongside the building, and I checked my jean's pocket and found a dime for admission and an extra nickel to buy a big sour pickle from the barrel in the lobby.

The name of the movie was *The Thing From Another World*. We all watched, wide-eyed, with fear and excitement, and

Homespun

jumped out of our seats in unison, screaming along with everyone else in the crowded theater when the Thing came on screen. The faces on the screen were so much bigger than real life, and I forgot the pain of the pickle juice dripping into the cuts on my fingers.

After the movie, we all huddled together in a group circle, walking as one person. The older boys were acting brave and talking loudly about the movie, saying how they weren't scared at all! Meanwhile, they kept me and the girls encircled as we started down Town Hill. We were halfway down when suddenly, Billy shouted, "Wait! We forgot our bikes!" Oh man! Everyone was so scared that we walked halfway home before we realized that we had forgotten the bikes!

Off we ran, back up the hill and through the square to where we had left the bikes. The movie house marquis lights were off now, and everything looked dark and scary—no cars or people to be seen anywhere. Everyone doubled up, and we rode as fast as we could toward home. I rode on the handlebars with my feet on the front fender as we sped down Town Hill. Squinting my eyes against the wind, I didn't dare let go of the handlebars to wipe the sweat from my face. As we approached the hairpin turn to cross the bridge over the creek, the mist was rising from the water and partially obscured the road. I hung on for dear life screaming as we took the turn, expecting at any moment for the Thing to appear and block our escape from the movie house.

The road leveled out, street lights became visible and marked the way, and everyone quieted down as the comfort of the sleepy neighborhood, familiar and safe, surrounded us like the hug of a favorite aunt.

Stories from that night would be told many times over, always debating who had been brave and who had been scared. As for me, I had been scared; frightened out of my mind—and I loved it! I was hooked for life. It was scary movies for me from that night on. Even now!

Years later, I returned to the old small town neighborhood. So much had changed. The houses were badly in need of care, the movie theater was gone, and sadly, so was Billy. His older brother, Jimmy, was driving him home from a Wednesday night prayer meeting, and they crashed into a telephone pole. Billy died instantly.

Before returning home, I took one last walk over the stone bridge, and memories flooded my mind as a broad smile crept across my face. I looked up to the sky and shouted, "Hey Billy! Thanks for the ride."

Swimming Lesson

It was the summer of '49 in the middle of a heat wave, or so I was told. All of the high school age boys from our house and the neighborhood were going swimming. I was just six years old and would be in the second grade next fall. I had never tried swimming before and didn't know how to swim, but I wanted to go.

I started begging and pleading, but to no avail, as Granny had not yet said yes and was still thinking about it.

Finally, Uncle Sonny stepped up and said, "Aw, Ma, he can come. I'll watch him." Granny said yes and I shouted yay!

So, off we went. Uncle Phil came too, along with the three Meyers brothers—Jim, Billy, and Tommy. We all piled into Granddaddy's Chevy pickup truck, and Uncle Sonny drove us up into the mountains by the upper region of the Conococheague Creek, with rolling hills of tall pine, river maple, and oak trees.

We parked in a clearing just off the dirt road and walked to a rocky outcropping about ten or twelve feet above the creek.

A huge limb of an old oak tree hung out over the gorge above the water where it flowed into a deep pool. A thick rope was tied to the limb, and everyone was excited and getting undressed at the same time.

We were going skinny dipping! What else? None of us owned a bathing suit anyway.

We lined up, waiting our turn to use the rope swing. Uncle Sonny picked me up in one arm, held me tightly to his chest, put his foot into the loop tied at the bottom of the rope, and off we flew into the air. Out over the river and back again. Out again, back again, going higher and higher each time. Finally, at the highest point, he let go. We flew into the air, yelling and laughing. As we hit the water, the cold took my breath away, and we sank below the surface.

I was gasping for air as we came back up, and Uncle Sonny swam us back to shore where we climbed the steep bank to do it again.

By the third time, I told Uncle Sonny I wanted to go by myself. He asked me, "Do you know how to swim?" I said, "No, I don't." He just laughed and asked, "Can you move your hands and feet at the same time?" I said, "Yes, but…"

We were already on the rope again. Out and back, and out and back, and then he threw me into the air—alone! I was screaming as I hit the water. When I reached the surface, he was a little more than arm's length from me, laughing and smiling and telling me to keep moving and swim over to him. He kept moving away from me, and I kept trying to reach him.

Suddenly, my feet hit the creek bottom, and I stood up. I had made it all the way back to the water's edge. I was out of breath, but all Uncle Sonny said was, "See, I told you, you could swim!"

We went again and again that afternoon. Uncle Sonny would go first and then wait for me to go all by myself. That was my first and only swimming lesson.

Late in the afternoon, we all pulled on our pants and ate a lunch made of cold country ham sandwiches on freshly baked bread with butter, washed down with cool water from our canteens, followed by fresh peaches canned from last summer.

The sun was sinking low in the sky, casting shadows across the water, when we piled back into the pickup truck for the drive home. I fell asleep within minutes, barely aware of Uncle Sonny covering me with his shirt, and woke already back home with the boys unloading the truck.

I was feeling very proud and brave as I tried to tell everyone about my swimming lesson, but I fell asleep once again, sitting upright in my chair at the table, unable to finish my supper.

Since I already had a bath, I was put to bed right away and dreamed all night about Uncle Sonny throwing me into the air, screaming and laughing as I hit the water below.

Sometimes, I still hear his laughter as he called out to me, "See, I told you, you could swim."

He was right!

Tough Guy

Harry Samuel Carter Jr. That was his full name, but to me, and all who knew him, he was Juni, or Uncle Juni.

During the late 1940s and 1950s, he was the chief detective for the Western Maryland Railroad, always inspecting the freight yards and the freight cars for stowaways or any type of criminal activity.

Sometimes he would discover individuals or entire families who were simply trying to find shelter for the night, or a way to travel to another town to seek employment and a fresh start in life. He directed these folks to the Salvation Army or other community services groups for help. No arrest necessary here.

Too often, however, under the cover of darkness, groups of men would drive their pickup trucks over back roads, headlights off, getting as close to the freight cars as possible, and unload the goods being shipped, loading them into their trucks. They were stealing. They were thieves and outlaws.

Uncle Juni caught and arrested most of them and often said he was glad he never had to use the .45 pistol he carried in a shoulder holster under his jacket. He stood six feet tall, was broad-shouldered and thick-chested, with strong hands, and short curly sandy-colored hair and grey eyes. Any who resisted, as all who worked with him agreed, were quickly subdued and taken into custody.

After school on this still warm September day, me and my friends—Johnny, Tommy, and Dubbie, third graders all—were playing where we were not supposed to be. In the freight yards!

We were close to the roundhouse where the giant steam engines could be repaired, inspected, and turned around to go in another direction. Each of the drive wheels was bigger than any of us. We climbed in and out of the open cars and, as we ran between them, we released the airbrake line used to couple the cars together. It made a loud hissing noise, and we all ran away down the never-ending line of cars.

Suddenly, there was a loud crashing sound as the cars moved backward and coupled together. A huge engine had just backed into them, preparing to move the massive train loaded with coal.

What the four of us heard was a scream. Dubbie was scared stiff, looking down at his left foot. The front of his shoe had been completely cut off, but no blood. I yelled, "No blood."

Dubbie had been wearing hand-me-down shoes at least a full size too big. Lucky!

Railroad men were running toward us now with Uncle Juni in the lead. He grabbed me firmly by both shoulders, pulled my face close to his, and yelled, "Ronnie, don't you ever come here again! You could have been killed. You understand me?"

Uncle Juni looked scared, and he was never scared of anything. Then I realized he was scared for me. Worried about me.

As we were sent home, Uncle Juni softened just a little. With a hint of a smile, he exhaled and said, "If you want to come see the trains, just ask me, and I will bring you."

And he did! The very next weekend.

How vivid these memories are now. Now, when I am a middle-aged adult, here with all of our family, waiting to serve as a pallbearer for my uncle Juni. Half the town had turned out for the funeral as, after retiring from the railroad, Uncle Juni became the best known motorcycle cop in the small town. School kids, businessmen, and housewives, all knew Uncle Juni—the motorcycle cop. When he rode through town, all was well. All was safe.

I walked through the funeral home, toward the door to the viewing area, and could just make out a figure standing silently by Uncle Juni's open coffin. It was his brother Alvey, eyes open, lost in trance-like thought and memory.

I knew this story; this connection. I had heard it several times from other family members after the war. And Uncle Alvey was remembering it.

It was D-Day plus six. Uncle Alvey was driving his jeep over shell-torn roads and terrain, taking written orders from the CO of his company to the command post of the forward most position of the ground troops pushing inland. After delivering the orders, he climbed back into his jeep and was about to return when he thought he saw a familiar figure or movement. A battle-worn face turned his way, and it was Uncle Juni's!

Constant heavy artillery fire made it hard to hear, so he leaped out of his jeep and ran over the crater-filled ground yelling, "Juni! Juni! Juni!"

No answer, so he yelled again, "Sergeant Carter!" Finally, Juni turned to look back.

They both smiled, laughed, and cried as they hugged each other on the battlefield. Alvey kept asking, "You okay? You all right?"

Juni kept answering, "Yes! I'm okay, I'm okay."

Juni's platoon was moving forward now. He and Alvey quickly shook hands. The small arms fire was increasing and was much closer, much louder.

Juni led the way, shouting the order to fix bayonets. This was going to get up close and deadly. He called back over his shoulder to Alvey, "Write Mom and Pop. Tell 'em I'm okay."

Alvey yelled okay, but Juni was already out of sight, leading the ground surge forward.

They parted, not knowing if they would ever see each other again.

From my position by the door, I watched Uncle Alvey's eyes return to the present. He reached down and patted Uncle Juni's shoulder and turned to leave. I slipped quietly away, not wanting to intrude on that moment. This was their memory; one that can only be shared with another soldier. I never mentioned it, but I felt privileged to have observed it. They were brothers at birth, brothers in arms, and brothers for life.

I waited by the coffin, thinking that surely God could always use another tough guy in heaven. Once again, as the first member of our family to pass on, Uncle Juni was doing what he did best. He was leading the way.

Tough guy!

Brother Jerry

She said it! She really did. Granny told me that I was going to meet someone today for the first time, and we would spend the day together.

But this person was my younger brother! What brother? I didn't know I had a brother! And I was not at all sure that I wanted a brother.

I was the youngest in the household and treated by my aunts and uncles as their little brother. Granny, Granddaddy, two aunts, and two uncles who were still in school, and me. That's how I liked it. The idea of having a younger brother was very confusing to me, and I wasn't sure I wanted one either.

I waited out back on the porch thinking that our well-tended vegetable garden seemed so small after leaving the farm last year and moving into town.

It was mid-July, the summer before I would enter the fourth grade, and a perfect day to be outside. My only chores now were to help with the garden, a chicken coop, and a hog pen out back. I had gathered the eggs, slopped the hogs, and weeded the garden before breakfast. Now, I just had to sit and wait.

I heard a car door close out front and, a minute later, I looked up to see Granny walking a skinny little boy back to meet me. He had a single long blonde curl running the full length of his head, and he wore freshly ironed dark blue short pants and a white short-sleeved shirt, with black sneakers and blue socks. I was in my bare feet, and wore blue jeans and a white T-shirt. Neither of us knew what to do or say, so I just said, "Hi, my name is Ronnie."

He answered, "Hi, my name is Jerry." We shook hands.

Granny said, "Go play," and took his small cardboard suitcase into the kitchen.

"We'll go down to the creek!" I yelled, and Granny called back, "Be home for supper!"

On the way out through the backyard, I grabbed a potato sack, put in four fresh ears of corn, four large red ripe tomatoes, and a box of barn burner matches for a fire. I put my fish knife in my back pocket. I told Jerry to grab two fishing poles from the washhouse and be careful not to tangle the lines or get caught on the sharp fish hooks.

Off we went, my sack slung over my shoulder, following my favorite path which wound out of the backyard, across the open field, and entered into the thick shaded woods. Here the sun shone through the trees in long narrow shafts of light, streaming and gleaming on their journey to reach the ground.

Soon we came to my hideaway spot, a huge old oak tree spreading over a deep gorge which led directly down to the Conococheague Creek. I reached in under its partly hollowed out roots and pulled out my steel cooking pot and cast iron skillet. I came here often, year round, to spend time alone and explore the ever-changing shoreline and the creek.

Along the bank was a stony clearing, jutting into the water just above the natural stone dam which ran all the way to the opposite shore. We stopped here and just listened to the squirrels in the trees scolding us for disturbing them, the birds calling out a warning of our intrusion, and the sound of the creek as it flowed over the rocks and picked up speed on its journey to the mighty Potomac.

This was the place where I felt happy, safe, and completely free. I held no fear of being alone with the woodlands and the water. It was a good place to share with my newfound little brother.

We had not spoken much and did not feel the need. It seemed our mutual love for the land was bringing us closer, speaking to us, for us.

We waded over the dam to the middle of the creek and sat quietly on a large rock with our feet dangling in the cool water.

Finally, I asked if he was hungry. He laughed and said, "I'm always hungry."

I laughed back. "Good, me too. Let's build a fire and then we'll catch some fish." I knew where the deep pools were and catching fish was not a problem.

Perhaps having a little brother was not so bad after all.

Jerry had never built a fire nor had he caught or cleaned a fish, so I had fun showing him how. He caught on right away. We cleared a sandy, flat area for the fire, and gathered very small dry twigs along with larger branches for later.

I shaved some small, thin slivers of wood onto the ground and stacked them like a teepee over some dry leaves. With one barn burner, the fire began to burn, and we added wood until it was enough to break down later into hot coals.

We peeled the husk from the corn, put them in my pot with water from a spring flowing into the creek, and let it begin to heat up.

Next, we dug for worms. In no time we had a dozen fat squirmy ones. I showed him how to insert the hook into the worm and leave about an inch hanging over to squirm in the water.

We did not have fishing rods and reels, but rather seven-foot fishing poles with twelve feet of line attached. About a foot from the hook and lead sinker was tied a block of cork which kept the hook and bait from sinking to the creek bottom and getting tangled in rocks or debris.

I selected a spot where the sun would not cast our shadow across the deep pool, and we threw lines upstream and let the current carry the bait downstream. After just a few times, we had caught three "sunnies" and one catfish.

I used the fishing line as a stringer, threading it through their gills and out their mouths to carry them back to our fire which now needed more wood.

Now I showed Jerry how to cut off the head behind the gills, remove the fins, and gut the fish to remove the insides. Next, I scaled the fish and handed Jerry my knife. He did just great with the remaining two sunnies, and we released the catfish. We figured he would grow much bigger next summer.

I had learned that Jerry had been living with our aunt Mary, her husband, Lindsay, and their daughter, Linda. He was happy with them and did not know about having a brother either.

I fried the fish using my knife to turn them often so as not to burn them. We ate the corn, sliced the tomatoes like apples, and used our fingers to eat the delicious crispy pan-fried fish.

Thirsty, we drank from the spring, poured water on the fire, and then spent the rest of the lazy afternoon talking and getting to know each other, skipping stones on the water, and exploring the shoreline for a few miles.

It was getting hot, so I suggested we go for a swim. That's when Jerry told me he couldn't swim. I felt a little scared that I hadn't watched him more closely when we had crossed the rock dam. I promised him that the next time he came to visit, I would teach him to swim, but meanwhile, I had him walk by the edge of the creek only.

Days were long, but I could tell by the shadow of the trees across the water that it was time to head home. We stashed my pot and skillet and reached home just in time to see everyone washing up for supper.

Everyone—Granny, Granddaddy, Uncle Phil and Sonny, and Aunt Jean and Tempi-Glen—were all happy to see Jerry and gathered around to say hello. They all knew him. I was very confused again. I was the only one who just met him today.

After supper, everyone said good-bye to Jerry, and Granny told us that he was to walk up to town square to catch the street car that would take him home.

I protested. Why couldn't he stay? Why did he have to leave? Granny said. "Ronnie, he has to go now or he will miss his trolley."

With that, Granny gave Jerry a hug and sent him on his way. He went out the front gate, looked back over his shoulder at me, and walked down the road toward the stone bridge.

Granny just watched him silently, but then said, rather sadly, "Ronnie, he's a good boy."

I watched him until he was almost out of sight, just a small skinny figure with his head looking down; his shoulders hunched forward and that little cardboard suitcase clutched in his hand.

What was I doing? What was I thinking? He was my little brother! I found myself running after him as fast as I could and caught him just before he reached the bridge. Breathless, I put my arm around his shoulders and took the suitcase from his hand. I told him I would walk him to the trolley stop and not to worry about anything—ever. From that very moment, we were bonded as brothers.

By the next summer, we would be living together under very different circumstances. Gone were the open fields, the dark shaded woods, the rolling hills and mountains, and the meandering creeks and streams of our young lives. We would grow to manhood, lead very exciting lives, and become very different people. Yet, we always remained committed to one another, and ready to help with any problem on a moment's notice, even when sometimes living half a world apart.

In the end, we would follow the pathway of our uncles: brothers at birth, brothers in arms, and brothers for life.

My brother, Jerry, as of this writing, is still with us; a colorful character fiercely proud of his independence and personal freedom. Driving an eighteen-wheeler, content and happy to live alone, he remains absolutely fearless in living his life as he chooses, yet always remains ready to give his moral support to me and my family if ever needed.

My only wish for my brother, Jerry, is one which has eluded him throughout his life.

Peace little brother. Peace.

You have done enough!

Sweet Sour Cherry Pie

It's true. I had noticed the twin high-backed black leather chairs before but no one seemed to sit in them—ever!.

They sat, side by side, on a round multi-colored area rug, facing toward the large bay window in the front of the house. Separating them was a narrow, highly polished, rectangular, black walnut end table with a pristine white doily draped across the center.

The window trim as well as the sills and sashes were painted a glossy white, and there were no curtains or blinds to obstruct the view through the spotlessly clean glass.

For some reason, on this day after school, I chose to kneel on the floor and play with my toy soldiers using the chair seats as my battleground.

Not for long. My aunt Jean, who would graduate high school that year, let me know very quickly that these chairs were special. They were for Granny and Granddaddy only.

That was fine with me, so I moved my toy soldiers to the hardwood floor in the dining room and played until supper time.

Supper was always special as Granny was a truly amazing cook, but tonight would be extra special because Granddaddy had asked for his favorite dessert: freshly baked sour cherry pie, with cherries canned over the summer and just enough sugar added to mellow the taste. So he called it—sweet sour cherry pie.

After saying grace and eating pot roast slowly roasted with onions, celery, carrots, and potatoes, served with freshly baked bread and butter, we all enjoyed a slice of pie. Granddaddy had two slices.

Then, in between homework, damping and rolling clothes for tomorrow's ironing day, and Granddaddy's bible reading, all seven of us played "Hide the Thimble." I was asked to hide the thimble while everyone else put their head down or covered their eyes. The thimble had to be hidden in plain sight, or at least be visible. After it was hidden, I called out, "Hot butter beans, come to supper!" and everyone began trying to find the thimble. When someone got close to the hiding place, I would yell, "Your hot!" or "Getting hotter!"

If they walked farther away, I would yell, "Now you're cold!" Finally, it was found by Uncle Phil, and it was his turn to hide it for the next round.

Soon, it was bedtime, and not long afterwards, I could hear Uncle Sonny and Uncle Phil breathing deeply as they slept in the double bed on the other side of our shared bedroom.

I was not sleepy tonight because I couldn't stop thinking about how good the pie had been. I wanted another piece, so I quietly got out of bed in my bare feet, put on my T-shirt, and crept downstairs.

The stairs ended at the back of the dining room where it joined the kitchen at the back of the house. I needed no light as the harvest moon was shining so brightly through the windows that I could make out colors and shadows.

I walked to the cupboard, quietly opened the door, and took out the pie. I was allowed to do this; just never take the last piece of anything, and don't make noise in the middle of the night.

I grabbed a fork, put a slice of pie on a saucer, and was enjoying my last bite when I thought I heard something in the front room. With the moonlight flooding through the windows, I could see someone was in the high-backed chairs.

It was Granny and Granddaddy, barely visible, sitting quietly. She was drinking a cup of hot tea, and he was drinking a cup of hot water with crushed up saltine crackers to settle his sometime ailing stomach.

Granny spoke quietly and said, "Harry, I will need a few extra things from the store this week."

As she placed her cup and saucer down on the table, Granddaddy reached over and placed his hand on top of hers. "Ann, whatever you need will be just fine."

Granddaddy's voice sounded different; it was softer, almost reverent as he spoke her name. Granny reached over and placed her other hand on top of his. Granddaddy leaned down slowly and kissed her hand. Then they simply returned to sitting together quietly in the soft semi-darkness.

I tip-toed back upstairs and crawled under my warm blankets, too young to understand why what I had just seen made me feel happy and peaceful. I felt safe.

Several happy decades followed with college graduations, new careers, marriages, newborn babies, and the annual Carter family reunion in July followed by the family Christmas party and dinner in December.

Our family was spread out now and some would travel many hours or even days to attend the reunions. Each family would bring their favorite specially prepared food dish along with all kinds of made-from-scratch cakes, pies, cookies, and candies. We would talk, laugh at old stories, play horseshoes and softball, and feast all day.

But, this year, as our nation celebrated its two hundredth anniversary, things were very different for our family. Granddaddy passed away four years ago and that sobered us all, and now the unthinkable had happened. Granny died today. Just three months shy of her ninetieth birthday.

Homespun

She died on her own terms, at home, in her own bed, surrounded by her loving family and friends. I can still feel her last hug as she told me good-bye. What a remarkable, strong, generous, and loving woman she was.

Three days later in the chapel filled to capacity with our family alone, Pastor Franklin, a long-time family friend, delivered his eulogy. With a reminder that Granny's story was one we needed to hear collectively and remember just one more time; this one last time, Pastor Franklin began.

Pastor Franklin spoke of her life's choices, beginning with how she gave up her inheritance, along with a century-old established family name with wealth and social position, to run away with and marry a penniless young farmer.

Granny traveled with Granddaddy by horse and buggy all the way from the Great Smoky Mountains in Tennessee to Washington County, Maryland. Here, they began farming just over 250 acres and started a family. Through the Great Depression, they worked the farm using two draft horses. No power equipment, electricity, or indoor plumbing was available.

Still, even during the worst of economic times, they would find ways to prosper and help those less fortunate with weekly charity offerings through their church. They would send four of their sons and three grandsons to fight wars on foreign soil. All the fourteen children Granny bore would grow to be strong, independent people with established careers, homes, and families of their own.

Ann's and Harry's lives were never about the pursuit of material wealth, social position, or power, but rather the strength of family unity.

Amen, Pastor Franklin.

Among many other things they lived to see were the coming of the automobile, electricity in homes, indoor plumbing, TV, air travel, and the landing of a man on the moon. Their world changed, quickly and radically, yet they stood together as a rock to which we were all firmly anchored.

After the burial, I stopped by Granny's house and everything—furniture, silver flatware, lamps, tables, chairs—everything was already gone, divided amongst family members. Even the matching high-backed black leather chairs had vanished and were never seen again.

I overheard a distant cousin remarked, as he looked around the empty house, that he didn't realize Granny and Granddaddy had been poor. I said nothing, but knew differently. They had been truly rich with all the things that money can never buy. I alone had the perfect memory, never shared with anyone. With the moonlight shining through the bay window, the chairs placed side by side, Granddaddy kissed Granny's hand, spoke her name, and in that moment, summed up their lives together. Committed. Priceless!

Just a few hours had passed since Granny's funeral yet, as I lay down for the last time in my old room, on my old pillow, and slowly drift off to sleep, I find I am neither happy nor sad, but strangely content. What a life they had led!

Soon I would enjoy happy dreams and memories, while smiling to myself as the night air slowly filled my room with the unmistakable aroma of sweet sour cherry pie.

The Beat Goes On

"Merry Christmas from the middle of the Mediterranean Sea!" That's what it said on the letter dated December 25, 1943, but I did not see this valued keepsake until my sixth birthday, January 10, 1949. Granny had been looking through some old mementoes and decided to share this one with me. It was addressed to Mom and Pop, telling them not to worry, and that he was fine. It was signed, "Your loving son, Eddie."

Serious details about exact location, names of ships, size of the fleet, or destination could not be written in any letter to be sent back home. Years later, we learned that Uncle Eddie's destroyer had been struck amid ship by two enemy torpedoes. It exploded, broke in half, and sunk very quickly. On that Christmas Day, the rescue boats from the fleet would need a full day to rescue survivors from the water. Uncle Eddie received a medal for staying with several wounded sailors, keeping them afloat and binding up their wounds until they could be rescued.

Thirteen months later, February 4, 1945, he was on another destroyer leading a small, secret battle group to protect President Roosevelt while he attended the famous meeting with the Allied Powers on the island of Malta. We would win the war and the world was being divided up.

After the war, Uncle Eddie gave his medal to Granny and never spoke of it again, except on rare occasions when he and his brothers would drift into a private conversation away from other family members during reunions. Veterans are like that sometimes.

After Pearl Harbor, Uncle Eddie and his brothers enlisted in the military and, within a few months, were trained and shipped overseas. They left not knowing how long the war would last, or if we could win.

I was glad Granny told me about Uncle Eddie, but now I wanted to go outside and play. The snow had been deep this winter and Granddaddy used the tractor with a plow attached to clear the driveway down to the main road. Sledding down the big hill beside the apple orchard with some other neighborhood kids, I noticed a shiny new green pickup truck turning into our driveway. I ran to meet it and sitting behind the wheel, smiling at me, was Uncle Eddie.

He wound down the window and I called out, "Wow! What a great truck. How can you drive in all this snow?"

He laughed and said, "Look, I've got snow chains on all four wheels." He asked if I would like to steer while he shifted the gears. I jumped into the truck, onto his lap, and steered all the way up the driveway to the front of the house. He gave it just enough gas to spin the wheels and fishtail just a little bit. It was scary and exciting at the same time.

Now, my Uncle Eddie was not just a handsome man, but movie star handsome. Everyone thought so, and he was very popular with the ladies, yet he was never conceited about it. He was average height with black wavy hair, a great smile with deep dimples, and an athletic build. In fact, he was very good at baseball and received an invitation to try out for the Brooklyn Dodgers. A terrible injury from a wild pitch severely damaged his left eye that ended his hopes for a professional sports career.

Undaunted, he started a hardware and electrical supply store with money he had been saving since the war. His business flourished because of his experience in the navy and his reputation for honesty. Soon after, Eddie met and married a sweet and lovely woman several years his senior. Her name was Roberta. She was a widow with two teenage daughters, Katherine and Cheryl. Eddie called his wife "Birdie" and he loved his new family very much.

Before their second anniversary, Birdie was diagnosed with cancer and died within six months. I was newly enlisted in the army but received an emergency hardship leave to attend the funeral of a relative. When I arrived in full-dress uniform, Uncle Eddie burst into tears as he hugged me and thanked me for coming.

He was the firstborn son, the last to marry, and now, he was a widower after just two short years. And a single parent! Uncle Eddie finished building what was to be their new home and cared for Birdie's two daughters until they completed high school and were off to college. Both girls were married within two years and moved to other parts of the country, losing contact with our family.

Feeling alone, Uncle Eddie stayed active and sold the house he had built. He purchased the old family farmhouse on Hospital Hill. He added updated electrical wiring, indoor plumbing, and kitchen appliances. The rest remained the same, and this would be the location of our family reunions for many years.

By my twenty-first birthday, the family was concerned that no male child had been born to carry on the Carter family name. All five of the brothers had married. Three of their wives could not bear children, one had two daughters, and Uncle Eddie was a widower. Of course, the family loved the girls, but having no male to carry on Granddaddy's name was a very real concern.

And then it happened! Uncle Eddie met a younger woman named Rebecca. They had a whirlwind courtship and, six months later, they married. Eighteen months after their marriage, Rebecca gave birth to a son. They named him David, and the Carter name would continue for another generation.

By the time Davy was two years old, Rebecca fell into a diabetic coma and died within a few days. Uncle Eddie was a widower again, with a young son to raise. He would never marry again, and Davy became the center of his life and world. They were always seen about town together. In time after high school and college, Davy was happily married and presented a grandson to Uncle Eddie.

The Carter name would go on; life would go on.

At the family reunions each July, I could see that age and poor health were upon Uncle Eddie. Yet, his smile, ready handshake, and sense of humor, remained the same.

Uncle Eddie sold his business and the old family home on Hospital Hill. But Uncle Eddie was not a man to remain idle. He took a position at the local hunting and fishing license and supply store and moved into an apartment only a block away. Each morning, Davy would stop by at 6:00 a.m., check on his father, and walk with him to work. Usually they didn't talk much, just spent time together and, of course, told stories about Eddie's grandson, little James.

The morning Davy had been dreading arrived with a beautiful sunrise and a cloudless sky. He entered the apartment. He heard no sounds of movement and did not smell the usual fresh brewed coffee. He knew what he would find in his father's bedroom.

Uncle Eddie had died quietly in his sleep. His great heart just stopped beating. He was the epitome of why his was considered our greatest generation. He never gave up or blamed any misfortune in his life on unfair or unjust circumstances. He never quit, never stopped living his life. His heart had stopped, but this blood would go on flowing through the heart of his son and grandson.

Because of Uncle Eddie's character, strength, and courage, the beat goes on…and on…and on. I am a better man for having known him. It was an honor.

Unfinished Symphony

Breakfast! Granny called out from downstairs. I could hear Aunt Jean and Aunt Tempi-Glen already setting the table so everyone could eat breakfast together. This was a big day, the first day of school, and my first day ever!

I rolled over in my bed and could see my two uncles—Phil and Sonny—throwing off the blankets on the big bed they shared. Without moving, Uncle Phil jumped to his knees and threw a pillow across the room, hitting me in the head.

That did it! I leaped to the center of the room, a pillow in each hand, and the battle was on. Uncle Sonny joined in and soon I was hit with so many pillows, I sank to my knees in the middle of the room. I was outmatched but not ready to give up. I ran back to my bed, jumped up onto the mattress, and turned, pillows in hand, to fight again. Uncle Phil threw a pillow, side-armed, that hit me in the chest so hard, it knocked me off the bed, onto the floor, and into the wall.

This was so great! I was about to go again when Granny's voice came through loud and clear. "Sonny, Phil, don't you hurt that boy. Get dressed and come down to breakfast."

Everything stopped right away but, as we were leaving the room, Uncle Phil reached back with one hand and grabbed me under the arm. He lifted me up, almost to the ceiling, and tossed me back to the center of my mattress. Those two strong healthy high school boys did this to me almost daily. I was not quite six years old, but I loved to roughhouse with them. I would turn out to be a very tough little kid.

After breakfast, we walked the five miles to my elementary school where they dropped me off before continuing to walk the last half mile to their high school.

Now, I know I was told that I had to go to school, but no one ever thought to tell me why. By lunchtime and recess, I'd pretty much decided that I'd had enough of being cooped up in school for one day. So, without telling anyone, I left the schoolyard. It was a beautiful, sunny September day, and I headed down Town Hill to the creek.

It was 3:00 p.m., time to go home, when they discovered I was missing. Telephone calls went out to Granny's house. When Uncle Phil and the others came by the school to walk me home, they were told I was missing. Uncle Phil seemed to know right away what was up. He told his brother and sisters to go home and tell Granny not to worry. He knew me; he knew where I would be.

I had my shoes off and my pants rolled up, wading in the creek, when Uncle Phil called out to me, "Ronnie, get out of that creek and come over here right now!"

Right there, as I put on my socks and shoes, he told me in a voice I had never heard before that this behavior could never happen again! I had never seen or heard Uncle Phil mad at me. I started to cry, but still I asked him why I had to go to school. He simply said, "Ronnie, you will need to grow up and be a strong man, and school will help teach you how."

When we got home, Granny was just about to fuss me when Uncle Phil said, "Don't bother, Mom. He won't do it again." Then, looking at me, he said, "Right, Ronnie?"

I answered, "Yes sir." I never forgot that lesson.

As if overnight, everyone graduated from high school. Aunt Jean went to Divinity College and Tempi-Glen took shorthand and typing classes. Uncle Sonny joined the army and Uncle Phil changed from part time to full time at the brickyard. On his twenty-first birthday, Phil married Mary, his high school sweetheart. They had been together since their freshman year and were one of the happiest and most romantic couples anyone had ever known. Mary started as a bookkeeper with a growing construction company, eventually becoming their chief head accountant. Uncle

Phil would remain with the brickyard and become an expert in manufacturing custom design brick and stone.

Our country was at war again, and with Uncle Sonny already in Korea, Uncle Phil tried to enlist in the army. All of his four brothers had served and he wanted to do his part. It was not meant to be. The hearing in his right ear, damaged as a result of childhood illness, made him ineligible. He was very disappointed. Mary, however, was secretly happy he couldn't go off to war as she wanted to start a family and didn't want to worry about Uncle Phil's safety.

Within that same year, the doctors told Mary that she could never have children. She told Uncle Phil that same day. They cried, hugged each other, told everyone in the family, and moved on with their lives.

Uncle Phil, like Mary, loved children. Their house became a gathering place for kids in the neighborhood. He put up a basketball hoop in the front of his garage, and Mary helped the girls draw chalk patterns on the driveway to play hopscotch. At family reunions, Uncle Phil and Mary still looked like high school sweethearts, always smiling, still holding hands, and kissing each other hello or good-bye.

One summer, they actually double-dated with me at the Hager Drive-In Theater because I did not have my driver's permit yet. They were only ten years older than me. Later, Uncle Phil gave me his new Buick Roadmaster to use the night of my senior prom. What a great car! It had power steering, automatic transmission, white sidewall tires—the works! We became good friends over the next twenty years. Good times for all.

So, when the news came that Uncle Phil had a terrible cancer strike his body, it hit our family hard. Uncle Phil was only fifty-five years old. It was in his stomach, spreading to his lungs, and beginning to invade his heart. Every known treatment was tried, but to no avail. Within a year, Uncle Phil died with his beloved Mary holding his hand. I barely remember the funeral. It left me feeling, not so much sad, as angry. The youngest brother was the first one to pass away prematurely. It just did not sit well with me.

Two years later, I was finally able to experience an unexpected form of closure. Uncle Phil's wife, Mary, was also dying in the same hospital from the same disease—cancer. Mary never smoked, was never overweight, and always appeared happy and healthy. Why? How? I was there with other family members when Mary called us together to say good-bye. She seemed very peaceful; resigned. After a while, she managed a tired smile, told us she loved us all and said, "Goodnight. I'm going to see Phil now."

After everyone else had left the room, I walked over beside her bed, leaned down close to her ear, gently touched her arm and whispered softly, "Mary, when you see Uncle Phil, tell him I said hello."

I walked out feeling as though their ending could not—no, would not, be all there was for them. Uncle Phil, Aunt

Mary. You could not have one without the other. Two lives, two sudden, too short; an unfinished symphony.

Perhaps next time. Yes, next time.

This time. Perhaps now!

Epilogue

So many lessons learned. Chief among them may be understanding and knowing that no matter how dire the circumstances and problems in your life, if you place love and family unity above them, a solution will come.

Granny and granddaddy taught me to give my children the priceless gift of loving their mother and while encouraging them to succeed in their lives, have them understand that a kiss, truly given, is worth more than any retirement income!

I learned that simple pathway: God, country, family, provides a compass for a well lived life.

This generation taught me about having the courage to take responsibility for the mistakes I would make, be willing to make course corrections, and follow a path that brings honor and joy to my life.

At this time, only three of my aunts are still living: Jean, Tempi-Glen, and Elta Mae. All are living independently and stay in close contact with each other. They still have the ability to make me feel like a loved younger brother, especially my aunt Jean who is just five years my senior.

In the future, I plan to continue sharing this story about real people, real courage, and real love.